OCT 0 5 2018

W9-DEZ-672

Go West! Travel to the Wild Frontier

GO WEST: FIRST CONTACT WITH NATIVE NATIONS

Cynthia O'Brien

Crabtree Publishing Company
www.crabtreebooks.com

Crabtree Publishing Company
www.crabtreebooks.com

Author: Cynthia O'Brien

Consultant: Professor Patricia Loughlin,
    University of Central Oklahoma

Managing Editor: Tim Cooke

Designer: Lynne Lennon

Picture Manager: Sophie Mortimer

Design Manager: Keith Davis

Editorial Director: Lindsey Lowe

Project Coordinator: Kathy Middleton

Editor: Janine Deschenes

Proofreaders: Wendy Scavuzzo and Petrice Custance

Children's Publisher: Anne O'Daly

Production coordinator and Prepress techician: Tammy McGarr

Print coordinator: Katherine Bertie

Production coordinated by Brown Bear Books

Photographs:
Front Cover: **Bridgeman Art Library:** main; **Library of Congress:** br;
Shutterstock: tr.

Interior: **Alamy:** Lanmas 21; **Corbis:** 29, Bettmann 13cr, 25, Heritage
Images 6tl, Historical Picture Archive 11l, Tarker 22; **Law Professor
Blogs, LLC:** 29t; **Library of Congress:** 4, 5tl, 5b, 6br, 7, 10, 12, 14tr, 18, 23,
24b; **Shutterstock:** Everett historical 16tr, 24t, Anton Lopatin 11br,
Jim Parkin 17; **Topfoto:** The Granger Collection 13b, 14b, 19, 20, 28; **Yale
University:** 15, 16bl.

All other artwork and maps **Brown Bear Books Ltd.**

Brown Bear Books has made every attempt to contact the
copyright holder. If you have any information please contact
licensing@brownbearbooks.co.uk

Library and Archives Canada Cataloguing in Publication

O'Brien, Cynthia (Cynthia J.), author
    Go West : first contact with native nations / Cynthia O'Brien.

(Go West! travel to the wild frontier)
Includes index.
Issued in print and electronic formats.
ISBN 978-0-7787-2331-8 (bound).--ISBN 978-0-7787-2348-6
(paperback).--ISBN 978-1-4271-1737-3 (html)

    1. Indians of North America--West (U.S.)--History--19th
century--Juvenile literature. 2. Indians, Treatment of--United States-
-History--19th century--Juvenile literature. 3. Indian Removal,
1813-1903--Juvenile literature. 4. Indians of North America--First
contact with Europeans--West (U.S.)--Juvenile literature. 5. Frontier
and pioneer life--West (U.S.)--Juvenile literature. I. Title. II. Title:
First contact with native nations.

E78.W5O37 2016   j978'.02   C2015-907976-4
                                          C2015-907977-2

Library of Congress Cataloging-in-Publication Data

Names: O'Brien, Cynthia (Cynthia J.), author.
Title: Go west : first contact with Native nations / Cynthia O'Brien.
Description: New York, New York : Crabtree Publishing, [2016] |
    Series: Go West! Travel to the wild frontier | Includes index. |
    Description based on print version record and CIP data provided
    by publisher; resource not viewed.
Identifiers: LCCN 2015050658 (print) | LCCN 2015049888 (ebook) |
    ISBN 9781427117373 (electronic HTML) |
    ISBN 9780778723318 (reinforced library binding : alk. paper) |
    ISBN 9780778723486 (pbk. : alk. paper)
Subjects: LCSH: Indians of North America--West (U.S.)--First
    contact with Europeans--Juvenile literature. | Whites--West
    (U.S.)--Relations with Indians--Juvenile literature. | United
    States--Territorial expansion--Juvenile literature. | Indians of
    North America--West (U.S.)--Wars--Juvenile literature. | Indians,
    Treatment of--West (U.S.)--History--Juvenile literature. | Frontier
    and pioneer life--West (U.S.)--History--Juvenile literature.
Classification: LCC E78.W5 (print) | LCC E78.W5 O27 2016 (ebook)
    | DDC 978.004/97--dc23
LC record available at http://lccn.loc.gov/2015050658

Crabtree Publishing Company
www.crabtreebooks.com   1-800-387-7650

Printed in Canada/022016/IH20151223

**Published in Canada
Crabtree Publishing**
616 Welland Ave.
St. Catharines, Ontario
L2M 5V6

**Published in the United States
Crabtree Publishing**
PMB 59051
350 Fifth Avenue, 59th Floor
New York, New York 10118

**Published in the United Kingdom
Crabtree Publishing**
Maritime House
Basin Road North, Hove
BN41 1WR

**Published in Australia
Crabtree Publishing**
3 Charles Street
Coburg North
VIC, 3058

CONTENTS

A Century of Change

Native peoples lived throughout North America for thousands of years before European settlers arrived. Westward expansion by new settlers in the 1800s changed the lives of the Native nations forever.

EXPANDING THE TERRITORY

★ **US buys French territory**

★ **Jefferson aims to develop the West**

In the early 1800s, France and Spain owned much of the land west of the Mississippi. In 1803, President Thomas Jefferson bought the vast Louisiana Territory from France for $15 million. The purchase almost doubled the size of the United States. Jefferson hoped to profit from **resources** in the West, such as land, minerals, and fur. US expansion, however, was a threat to Native peoples in the West. They faced the prospect of losing their traditional lands.

DID YOU KNOW?

In 1845, the newspaper editor John O'Sullivan used the phrase "manifest destiny" to describe a belief that it was the right of the United States to take ownership of land in the West. Supporters of manifest destiny believed that the white government would benefit Native peoples. But it did them terrible harm.

Go West!

★ **Shaping the nation**

★ **Across the continent**

In 1812, Americans went to war with Britain, their former **colonial** ruler. The United States wanted to remove any foreign influence from their country. The war made Americans think about what sort of country they wanted to live in. Many began to believe they should impose their government across North America and over the Native nations who already lived in the West.

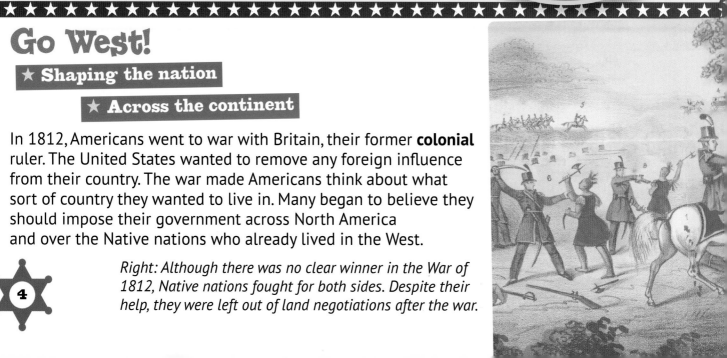

Right: Although there was no clear winner in the War of 1812, Native nations fought for both sides. Despite their help, they were left out of land negotiations after the war.

Claiming the Land

★ **Work the land for five years**

★ **Build a home and it's yours**

The US and Canadian governments were eager to encourage settlers to move to the West, especially to farm the Great Plains. In May 1862, President Lincoln signed the **Homestead** Act to make moving west more attractive. The act allowed any US citizen or immigrant to claim 160 acres (65 ha) of government land in the West for free. In Canada, the Dominion Lands Act of 1872 promised the same amount of land. However, these acts ignored that these lands were already occupied by First Nations.

The Iron Horse

★ **Transcontinental railroad completed**

★ **Lines meet in Utah**

In 1869, the Union Pacific and Central Pacific Railroads met in Utah, completing the first transcontinental railroad. Settlers built farms near the tracks and towns grew up. Native peoples called the railroad the "iron horse." For them, it was an unwelcome sign of change. The track crossed prime hunting lands. Native peoples, including the Northern Cheyenne, Sioux, and Arapaho, fought to try to defend their territory.

Right: Workers and company officials celebrate the completion of the transcontinental railroad at Promontory Summit, Utah, on May 10, 1869.

Ways of Life

Many different Native peoples lived in the West, from the Blackfoot in the North to the Navajo in the Southwest. Their lifestyles were shaped by their natural environment.

THE BUFFALO

* ★ **Versatile animal**
* ★ **Herds are key to survival**

On the plains, the buffalo was central to life. According to the beliefs of some Plains nations, the animal gave itself to the people. The people held ceremonies to celebrate the way it **sacrificed** itself for them. Every part of the buffalo was used, including its meat for food, and skins for making clothes. Its bones were used to make tools and its sinews to make thread.

Left: Native hunters use horses and bows and arrows to hunt buffalo.

Tribal Lands

* ★ **Traditional territories**
* ★ **US government imposes borders**

Native peoples had traditional territories. Some groups shared hunting lands, but others fought over territory. In the 1800s, the US government imposed borders on the West. In 1834, it set up Indian Territory (modern Oklahoma) for Native peoples. The nations already living there resented the arrival of new groups of Native peoples. The new arrivals resented being moved there against their will.

Right: Piegan Blackfoot tipis next to a pond on the northern plains.

HORSE NATION

★ **Horse introduced by Spanish**

★ **Expert Native riders**

The Spanish brought the first horses to North America from Europe in the 1500s. By the late 1700s, many Native nations had horses. Some, including the Comanche and Apache, were excellent horsemen. This made it easier to travel, and some tribes became more **nomadic**. Plains peoples used horses to hunt buffalo, and in warfare. By the 1800s, the horse had become essential to some nations' ways of life.

Right: The Kiowa warrior Elk Tongue sits on his war pony, wearing a headdress traditionally worn into battle.

From Place to Place

★ **Pack up and go!**

★ **Moving with the buffalo**

Some Plains nations followed the herds of buffalo that they hunted for food. The buffalo moved to different parts of the plains in summer and winter. The Plains nations could move their belongings easily. They could dismantle their cone-shaped tents, or **tipis**. They strapped the tents and other goods to an A-shaped wooden frame called a *travois*. The travois was pulled by a horse to the new hunting ground.

DID YOU KNOW?

Europeans called the wild animal of the plains the "buffalo," because it looked like the European water buffalo. In fact, the animal is a bison. It has short horns, a large head, and a thick mane.

FIELDS OF CORN

★ **Southern nations tend crops**

★ **Use traditional techniques**

Not all Native peoples were nomads. The Hopi, for example, built stone and **adobe** homes. They grew crops such as squash, corn, and beans, which grow well when planted together. Farther to the east, the Choctaw farmed in fertile river valleys. Families had small gardens but also helped to tend large communal fields. They dug the soil and planted the corn in rows. They planted squash, sunflowers, and watermelon between the rows of corn.

Where in the West?

Northwest Coast
The peoples of the Northwest Coast were skilled at fishing and trading. They hunted whales from canoes and fished for salmon.

Plateau
Peoples of the Plateau hunted large animals such as elk, and gathered plants and roots. They also fished in the region's many rivers.

Great Basin
Much of the Great Basin was dry and difficult to live in. Peoples lived beside lakes or rivers, or traveled to hunt animals and gather plants.

California
The ways of life for the peoples of California were different, depending on how close they were to the coast. On the coast, people used shells as a form of money. Inland, some peoples were expert basket weavers.

Southwest
The Southwest was home to nomadic peoples such as the Apache, and farming peoples such as the Navajo and the Pueblo. The Pueblo lived in villages of homes made from dried mud.

Coast Salish

Chippewa

CANADA

Cree

Chinook

Blackfoot

Yakima

Crow

Nez Percé

Modoc

Shoshone

Cheyenne

Arapaho

Paiute

Pawnee

Ute

Chumash

Navajo

Comanche

Pueblo

Apache

In 1800, Native peoples still dominated the West and much of the Southeast. Territories were loosely defined, however, and some nations ranged widely.

Cree

Ojibwa

Sioux

UNITED STATES

Shawnee

Natchez

Choctaw

Chickasaw

Creek

Cherokee

Seminole

Key

- Pacific Northwest
- California
- Great Basin
- Southwest
- Great Plains
- Southeast
- Plateau

Locator map

Plains

The vast grasslands of the Great Plains were home to numerous nations who depended on the huge herds of buffalo. Most peoples were semi-nomadic and followed the buffalo migration through the seasons.

Southeast

The Americans called the Native peoples of the Southeast—the Cherokee, Chickasaw, Choctaw, Creek, and Seminole—the "Five Civilized Tribes." This was because they adopted from the colonial Americans some practices such as forms of agriculture.

Native Peoples' Ways of Life

Native peoples had complex systems of social organization, spiritual beliefs, and religious rituals.

Traditional Roles

★ **Women do the work...**

... and so do the men!

In many Native groups, men and women had different roles. Women tended crops, prepared food, made clothing, and looked after children. They were also skilled at art, such as **beadwork**. Men hunted, fished, and fought in battle. In some Native groups, these roles were not as clearly defined. There were many female warriors, for example.

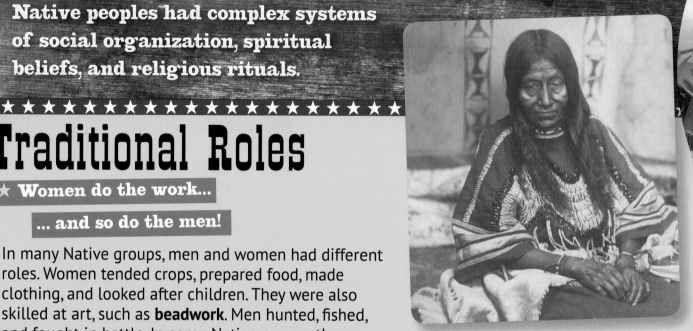

Above: A Piegan woman, Two Kill, sits on woven blankets. Women wove clothes from fur or wool.

Tribal Leaders

★ **Chiefs earn respect**

★ **Power of the shaman**

Both male and female **elders** had a voice in important tribal decisions. Elders advised younger tribe members about skills such as hunting. Although all elders had a say in tribal discussions, it was the tribe's chief who made the final decision. Some tribes had a special war chief to lead warriors in times of conflict. A tribe's spiritual leader was the **shaman** (left). Native peoples believed the shaman had a powerful, almost magical connection with nature. He or she was a healer, a teacher, and an advisor.

The Mandan buffalo dance, painted by Karl Bodmer in the early 1840s.

HUNTING RITUALS

★ Animals honored ...

... with dances and songs

Most Native Americans believed everything in nature was connected. They thought there was a special bond between hunters and their prey. Hunters held ceremonies to honor the animals that had given up their lives so the tribe could eat. The Mandan, for example, held an annual dance before the buffalo hunt. Men wore buffalo skins on their backs and painted their skin. They danced for three days to lure the buffalo to Mandan territory. After the buffalo returned on their annual migration, the Mandan held a large feast to give thanks.

DID YOU KNOW?

Native peoples traded using a system called bartering. Peoples exchanged goods such as furs, tobacco, wheat, and corn for goods they wanted. Some Native peoples also exchanged a string of shell beads called *wampum* as gifts to use in ceremonies or, later, as a type of currency.

WHAT'S ON THE MENU?

A Native American feast!

☞ **Buffalo Meat**
☞ **Squash**
☞ **Fresh Fish**
☞ **More Buffalo Meat**
☞ **Chokeberries**
☞ **Turnips**
☞ **Pemmican**
☞ **Elk Meat**
☞ **Corn**
☞ **Even More Buffalo Meat**

First Contact

The first contact many western Native peoples had with Americans came at the start of the 1800s, after the United States took control of the West.

Above: Chiefs of the Sioux, one of the largest tribes of the northern plains.

Beyond the Mississippi

★ **Varied landscapes ...**

... home to varied peoples

The grasslands, mountains, deserts, and coastlines west of the Mississippi were home to hundreds of thousands of Native Americans. The Plains peoples included the Pawnee and Arapaho nations. The now-Canadian plains included nations such as the Ojibwa and Cree. The Chinook and the Clatsop were two of the northwestern tribes, while the Navajo and Apache were among the larger southwestern groups.

MY WESTERN JOURNAL

Imagine you are one of the Native peoples who met Lewis and Clark on their expedition to the West. Would you welcome them, or be suspicious? Explain your reasons.

TWISTED VIEWS

★ **Native homes ignored**

Although the West was home to Native peoples in the early 1800s, there were no white settlements. The US government therefore considered this vast region to be "empty." White Americans believed their way of life was superior to the Native American ways. They regarded Native peoples as "savages." Americans felt it was their duty to impose their "superior" values and beliefs on Native peoples. One result of this was that the US government did not feel it had to stick to **treaties** it made with Native peoples.

Heading up the Missouri

★ Lewis and Clark head inland

★ Encounters with many nations

In 1804, President Thomas Jefferson sent Meriwether Lewis and William Clark to find a route to the Pacific Ocean by river. The explorers traveled up the Missouri River. Along the way they met the Oto, Missouri, Mandan, Nez Percé, and Clatsop peoples. Lewis and Clark were guided by Sacagawea, the Shoshone wife of a French-Canadian **fur trapper**. Sacagawea knew the land, and also how to find edible plants and roots.

THE FUR TRADE

★ Into the Canadian West

In Canada, First Nations became involved in the fur trade. There was a great demand for beaver fur in Europe, where it was used to make hats. European companies such as the Hudson's Bay Company and, later, the North West Company, set up trading posts, where First Nation and European trappers took their furs. European trappers often lived and worked with First Nations. Many married First Nations women and had families.

Sacagawea points the way for Lewis and Clark.

MAKING NEW CONTACTS

★ Soldier explores Arizona

In 1806, Zebulon Pike explored the southern part of the Louisiana Territory (left), where he met the Osage and Pawnee peoples. Pike stayed in a Pawnee village in Spanish territory for several weeks. He persuaded the Pawnee to fly a US flag instead of a Spanish flag. The Spanish eventually captured Pike but later released him.

The Government Takes Action

Throughout the **1800s**, the **United States** government passed a series of laws to try to control the **Native nations** and their territory.

WE WANT TO STAY

★ **Thousands forced to relocate**

★ **Nations driven from homelands**

In the early 1800s, the Cherokee, Choctaw, and other nations lived in the southeastern United States. The government wanted to give the land to white settlers, so it passed the Indian Removal Act in 1830. The act promised land in the West to the nations if they left the South. However, those who refused were forced to leave. By 1837, about 46,000 Native peoples had been **displaced** from their homelands.

Above: The warrior Tah-Chee was among the Cherokee who were forced to move.

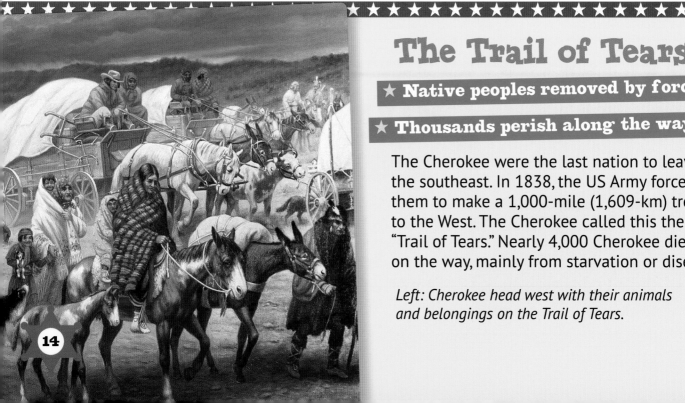

The Trail of Tears

★ **Native peoples removed by force**

★ **Thousands perish along the way**

The Cherokee were the last nation to leave the southeast. In 1838, the US Army forced them to make a 1,000-mile (1,609-km) trek to the West. The Cherokee called this the "Trail of Tears." Nearly 4,000 Cherokee died on the way, mainly from starvation or disease.

Left: Cherokee head west with their animals and belongings on the Trail of Tears.

Strangers in a Strange Land

★ Southern nations forced to adapt

★ Moving to Indian Territory

The US government sent the peoples of the Southeast to "Indian Territory" (modern-day Oklahoma). The plains landscape was strange to groups such as the Cherokee. They also spoke different languages and had different customs from the Plains nations. The arrival of more people on the plains meant there were fewer resources to go around. This caused resentment among nations living in the region. The newcomers found it difficult to rebuild their societies.

MY WESTERN JOURNAL

Imagine that you are a member of one of the "Five Civilized Tribes." Write a letter to the president of the United States to explain why your tribe should stay in the Southeast.

DID YOU KNOW?

The Canadian government passed the Indian Act in 1867. It laid out rules for Native nations to live on reservations under government control. During the process, Native land in the West was opened for European settlement.

RESISTANCE!

★ War with the Seminole

★ Fighting relocation

In 1817 and 1818, the US Army began to try to remove the Seminole from their land in the Southeast. After the United States gained Florida from Spain in 1821, the army intensified its campaign. The Seminole did not want to leave Florida. They moved south. In 1835, the US Army tried to move them from their new lands. After seven years of fighting, about 4,000 Seminole moved west, but a small number fled to the Florida Everglades. Most of the remaining people left after a third conflict in 1855.

Left: Seminole warriors attack a US Army fort in Florida in December 1835.

The Settlers Arrive

From the mid-1800s, new arrivals flooded into the West, from religious settlers to gold miners.

THE MORMONS MOVE TO UTAH

★ **Seeking freedom for religious beliefs**

★ **Destroyed freedom of Native peoples**

The Mormons arrived in the Salt Lake Valley in Utah in 1847. They were escaping religious **persecution** in the East. At first, the newcomers were friendly with the local Ute and Paiute peoples, but soon began to take over Native land. Then, Mormons passed a law allowing settlers to punish Native people who would not give up their resources. By 1869, 80,000 Mormons had arrived. Eventually, the Paiute and Ute were forced to move to **reservations**.

Above: Ute families imprisoned in Fort Utah after disobeying Mormon laws.

★ **Miners flock to California**

★ **Seize traditional Native lands**

Under Attack

When gold was discovered in California in January 1848, thousands of settlers arrived (left). Many mined on Native American land. In 1850, a new state law allowed settlers to force Native people into unpaid work. The state **militia** attacked native settlements that tried to resist. Native peoples lost most of their land. By 1860, the Native population of California had fallen from 150,000 to just 30,000.

A New Trail

★ Shortcut to Montana ...

... through Sioux hunting lands

The **mountain man** John Jacobs and his partner John Bozeman established the Bozeman Trail in 1863. It was a shortcut from the Oregon Trail, going north to the goldfields of Montana. The new trail passed through the Powder River Basin, which had been given to the Sioux as hunting land by the 1851 Treaty of Fort Laramie. The Sioux and their allies, the Arapaho, tried to protect their lands by attacking settlers on the trail. The US Army, breaking the treaty that promised this land to the Sioux, built three forts to try to protect the settlers.

DID YOU KNOW?

The Sioux tried to stop settlers crossing their hunting lands on the Bozeman Trail. The Lakota chief Red Cloud led a two-year campaign known as Red Cloud's War. In 1868, the land was returned to the Sioux and the trail was closed.

INTO SACRED LAND

★ Custer leads search for gold

★ US Army and Sioux go to war

The Black Hills of Dakota, or Paha Sapa, were sacred land for the Lakota Sioux. The government gave the land to the Sioux in the Treaty of Fort Laramie in 1868. However, in 1874, Lieutenant Colonel George Armstrong Custer led a large expedition into the Black Hills. They found gold, and thousands of miners rushed to the area. This led to fighting between the US military and the Sioux in the Great Sioux War of 1876. Eventually, the Sioux were overcome and forced to surrender. They were moved onto reservations. Today, the nation still fights for their rights to the Black Hills.

Right: The Black Hills were Sioux territory, but the government wanted them for gold.

New Neighbors

As settlement increased, Native peoples encountered the homesteaders, traders, and missionaries who settled in the West.

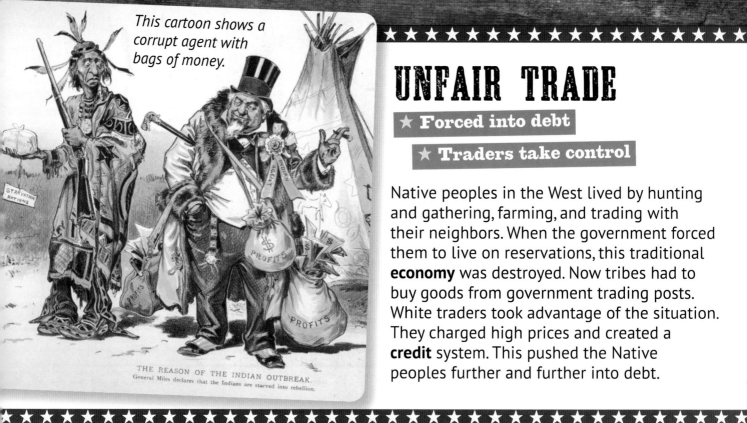

This cartoon shows a corrupt agent with bags of money.

THE REASON OF THE INDIAN OUTBREAK.
General Miles declares that the Indians are starved into rebellion.

UNFAIR TRADE

★ **Forced into debt**

★ **Traders take control**

Native peoples in the West lived by hunting and gathering, farming, and trading with their neighbors. When the government forced them to live on reservations, this traditional **economy** was destroyed. Now tribes had to buy goods from government trading posts. White traders took advantage of the situation. They charged high prices and created a **credit** system. This pushed the Native peoples further and further into debt.

DID YOU KNOW?

When cowboys drove cattle across Native land, nations often charged them. They took a few cattle as payment or charged a cash toll for each cow. Nations also charged settlers who used their land. They also sold them supplies such as wild game.

Crooked Dealers

★ **Taking advantage of Native peoples**

★ **We've been robbed!**

The US government sent agents to the reservations. The agents were supposed to help Native peoples by buying them food and clothing. Some of these agents were honest, but many were corrupt. They sold mineral and forestry rights on Native land to white settlers, but did not give the Native peoples the money. The government stopped using "Indian agents" in the early 1900s.

In the early 1800s, **missionaries** from various Christian churches moved west. They wanted to **convert** the Native Americans to Christianity, but also to "civilize" them. Missions were set up at trading posts, and mission schools were opened on reservations. Missionaries Samuel Allis and John Dunbar lived among the Pawnee for five months. Although many Native peoples listened to the missionaries, most did not convert. The nations already had their own customs and beliefs.

Left: The missionary Narcissa Whitman (right) looks after a sick member of the Cayuse at the Whitman Mission in California in the 1840s.

Raised by the Comanche

★ **Rescued woman wants to return**

In 1836, Comanche warriors attacked a white settlement in their territory in Texas. The warriors captured six people, including nine-year-old Cynthia Ann Parker. The Comanche named her Nadua, and she lived with them for 24 years. She married a chief and had three children. In 1860, Texas Rangers found Nadua (right) and her daughter Prairie Flower during a raid on a Comanche camp. Cynthia became famous for being rescued, but she wanted to return to the Comanche. Prairie Flower died of an illness in 1863. Cynthia died in 1870 without ever being reunited with her Comanche family.

The Loss of the Buffalo

The disappearance of the buffalo was one of the most devastating changes for Native peoples. For the nations who lived on the Great Plains, it marked the end of a whole way of life.

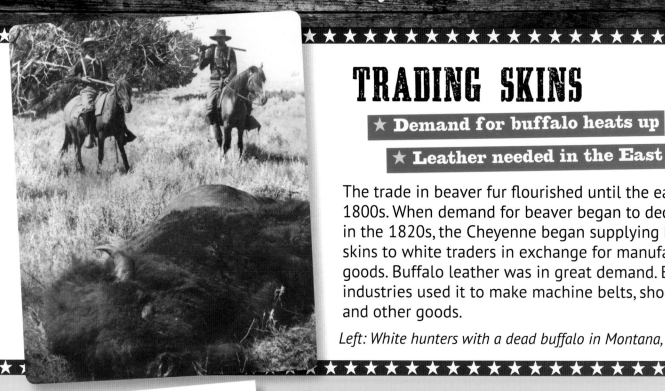

TRADING SKINS

★ **Demand for buffalo heats up**

★ **Leather needed in the East**

The trade in beaver fur flourished until the early 1800s. When demand for beaver began to decline in the 1820s, the Cheyenne began supplying buffalo skins to white traders in exchange for manufactured goods. Buffalo leather was in great demand. Eastern industries used it to make machine belts, shoes, and other goods.

Left: White hunters with a dead buffalo in Montana, 1882.

MY WESTERN JOURNAL

Write a poem about the buffalo and what it meant to the Plains peoples.

Hunting for Money

★ **Hunters hired to round up the buffalo**

★ **Millions made from bones**

The Plains peoples hunted the buffalo, but they never killed more animals than they needed to survive. By the 1860s, buffalo hunting was big business. Hired hunters, such as Buffalo Bill Cody, became famous. In just two years, white hunters killed millions of buffalo for their meat, skins, and bones, which were used to make fertilizer and glue.

WHERE ARE THE BUFFALO?

★ **Farms, railroads, and hunters to blame**

About 60 million buffalo roamed the plains in 1800. White settlement brought farms, ranches, towns, and railroads which disrupted the animal's habitat. Texas fever, a cattle disease, killed many buffalo, but far more were killed by hunters. By the end of the 1800s, there were fewer than 1,000 buffalo left on the plains.

Left: Buffalo flee from a hunting party carried to the plains by train.

DID YOU KNOW?

White hunters shot buffalo with new long-range rifles, which were accurate and fast. Railroads ran special trains where sport hunters could fire at buffalo spotted along the tracks.

A WAY OF LIFE VANISHES

★ **Plains peoples lose their customs**

The buffalo were central to the lives of the Plains peoples. Buffalo provided them with food, and with hides for clothing. They were also important to the religious beliefs and rituals of Native peoples. Peoples such as the Sioux fought to avoid being forced to live on reservations where they would not be able to hunt. Meanwhile, white hunters killed millions of buffalo. Even if Native peoples had been able to roam freely across the plains as they had in the past, there were no longer enough buffalo left to support them.

Lament for the Buffalo

Kicking Bird of the Kiowa tribe put into words his feelings about the loss of the buffalo: "Just as it makes a white man's heart feel to have his money carried away, so it makes us feel to see others killing and stealing our buffaloes, which are our cattle given to us by the Great Father above to provide us meat to eat and means to get things to wear."

The Coming of the Railroad

The railroad brought new waves of settlement to the West. For the Native peoples, the railroad was another symbol of destruction.

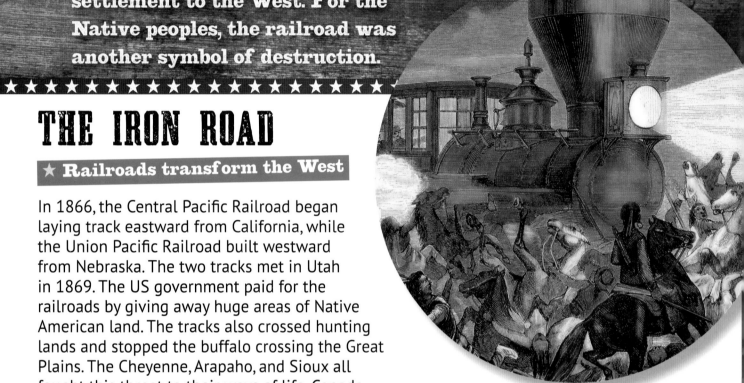

THE IRON ROAD

★ Railroads transform the West

In 1866, the Central Pacific Railroad began laying track eastward from California, while the Union Pacific Railroad built westward from Nebraska. The two tracks met in Utah in 1869. The US government paid for the railroads by giving away huge areas of Native American land. The tracks also crossed hunting lands and stopped the buffalo crossing the Great Plains. The Cheyenne, Arapaho, and Sioux all fought this threat to their ways of life. Canada completed the Canadian Pacific Railroad in 1885.

Above: This illustration from 1870 shows Native warriors attacking a railroad train.

DID YOU KNOW?

The Pawnee were one of the few tribes to welcome the railroad. The railroad company promised the Pawnee free rides. In return, the Pawnee helped guard the railroad crews and livestock from their traditional enemy, the Sioux.

Breaking Promises

★ Tribes give up land rights
★ Government ignores treaties

In 1868, the Treaty of Fort Laramie recognized Sioux ownership of the Black Hills. However, after gold was found there a few years later, the US government took the land anyway. This set a pattern. Whenever land became valuable for settlement, the government broke its agreements with Native peoples and took the land.

The Army Gets Involved

★ War hero leads peace talks

The railroad brought thousands of US Army soldiers into Native American territory. By the 1880s, the army had built 100 forts across the West. More than 15,000 soldiers were based there to guard settlers and railroad workers from Native American attacks. General William Sherman, a famous Civil War leader, helped **negotiate** peace treaties with Native peoples. However, the government soon broke the treaties.

Above: A group of Sioux elders during negotiations at Fort Laramie in 1868.

DON'T FENCE ME IN!

Below: The Laguna Reservation in New Mexico, home to the Pueblo, was crossed by the Santa Fe Railroad.

★ Freedom for settlers ...

... but not for Native peoples

The transcontinental railroad brought increased freedom for settlers heading west. It made what had been a long, dangerous journey across the country much quicker and safer. Merchants and traders used the trains to carry goods throughout the continent. In contrast, by the end of the 1880s, most Native Americans lived on reservations. They were no longer able to roam freely. Instead, the government wanted them to settle and grow wheat, and to eat the beef and other food the government supplied.

At War

During the 1800s, some Native peoples fought the US Army as they tried to defend their lands.

The Apache

★ Waging war for 25 years

The Apache people lived in the Southwest. In the late 1850s, they clashed with miners who moved into Apache territory in search of gold. In 1861, the US Army falsely accused the Apache leader Cochise of kidnapping the son of a white settler. The incident sparked a series of violent clashes. In 1872, Cochise agreed to stop fighting in return for land in Arizona. However, after he died in 1874, the government took the land back. The Apache leader Geronimo continued fighting the US Army, until he surrendered in 1886.

Above: Geronimo was a feared war leader of the Chiricahua Apache.

RED CLOUD'S WAR

★ Sioux protect territory

★ Treaty closes trail

The Sioux attacked travelers on the Bozeman Trail, which crossed their hunting lands. The army built forts to protect travelers. In December 1866, Sioux warriors led by Red Cloud killed 81 US soldiers under Captain William J. Fetterman in Wyoming (left). After more battles, Red Cloud agreed to the Treaty of Fort Laramie in 1868. The government agreed to close the Bozeman Trail.

GREAT SIOUX WAR

★ **Sioux ignore Grant's orders**

★ **Go to war with US Army**

The 1868 Treaty of Fort Laramie set aside land for the Great Sioux Reservation. Many Sioux continued to roam the plains to hunt buffalo. President Ulysses S. Grant told the Sioux to move to the reservation by January 31, 1876. The Sioux leader Sitting Bull encouraged his people to ignore the order. When US Army forces arrived, the Great Sioux War began. The two sides clashed in the Battle of the Rosebud on June 17, 1876, and in the Battle of the Little Bighorn on June 25. By early spring of 1877, US forces had the upper hand. The Sioux surrendered and unwillingly moved to the reservation.

*Above: Sioux leaders and their **interpreter** visit Washington, DC, to try to negotiate to keep their lands.*

DID YOU KNOW?

On June 25, 1876, General George Armstrong Custer and his Seventh Cavalry found Sitting Bull's village on the Little Bighorn River. Custer attacked, but met 2,000 Lakota Sioux, Northern Cheyenne, and Arapaho warriors led by Crazy Horse. Outnumbered, Custer and all his men died.

The California Wars

★ **Modoc rebels refuse to move**

★ **Captain Jack leads resistance**

The Modoc people clashed with settlers in northern California and Oregon. In 1864, the Modoc agreed to move to Klamath Reservation, Oregon. A small number of Modoc led by Kintpuash, known as Captain Jack, fled to a remote part of California. In 1872, the US Army arrived to force them onto the reservation. The soldiers defeated the Modoc and killed their leaders. The rest of the Modoc were sent to Indian Territory in modern-day Oklahoma.

A Changed Land

Blood Reserve

The Blood Reserve in Alberta is the largest First Nations reserve in Canada. It was established in 1877 under the terms of Treaty 7, made between Queen Victoria and the governments of Blackfoot First Nations, including the Blood (Kainai) and Siksika bands.

Siksika

Blood

Nez Percé

Blackfoot

Cheyenne

Shoshone

Sioux

Arapaho Shoshone

Ute

Ute

Navajo Hopi Zuni

Arapaho Cheyenne

Apache

Apache Comanche

Tongue River

The Northern Cheyenne were moved to a reservation in southern Montana. They were originally sent to Indian Territory with the related Southern Cheyenne, but many died from hunger and disease. In 1878, some Cheynne headed north. The government later created a reservation for them on the Tongue River.

Wind River

The reservation at Wind River in Wyoming was created for the Eastern Shoshone in 1868. It was also home to significant numbers of Arapaho.

Four Corners

The Four Corners region, where Colorado, Utah, Arizona, and New Mexico meet, was home to four reservations for the Navajo, Hopi, Ute, and Zuni.

26

By 1894, the Native peoples of the West had been forced to live on small reservations that made it difficult to maintain their ways of life.

CANADA

Key

Land reserved for Native Americans

Locator map

h ppewa

UNITED STATES

Pawnee
Cherokee
Creek
Choctaw
Chickasaw

Indian Territory
Indian Territory was created by the US government in 1834 as a place to send the "Five Civilized Tribes" of the Southeast. A number of Native peoples were forced to live there, even if they did not share similar cultures.

Great Sioux Reservation
The Treaty of Fort Laramie of 1868 created a large reservation for the Lakota Sioux in what is now South Dakota. Six years later, the government claimed part of the land for white settlement after gold was found in the Black Hills.

A Legacy of Settlement

As the 19th century closed, the Native American lands had disappeared. Towns and homesteads replaced traditional tribal territory.

THE DAWES ACT

⭐ **Government act breaks up reservations**

⭐ **One plot of land each**

The General Allotment Act, known as the Dawes Act, became law in 1887. It allowed the government to divide Native reservations into small plots for individuals or families from the tribe. The government kept or sold any "surplus," or leftover land—but it was often better quality than the land given away in the allotments. The act had the effect of taking away even more Native American land.

DID YOU KNOW?

The Dawes Act made almost 2 million acres (809,371 ha) of tribal lands available in Indian Territory. It was opened for white settlement on April 22, 1889. Up to 60,000 people raced to claim land. In 1907, the former Indian Territory became the state of Oklahoma.

Last Resistance

⭐ **New movement gives hope**

⭐ **Sioux killed at Wounded Knee**

In 1889, a Paiute **seer** named Wovoka had a **vision** that the plains would be returned to Native peoples if they performed a ritual dance. The dance spread quickly, alarming the authorities. On December 15, 1890, police killed the Lakota Sioux chief Sitting Bull. On December 28, US soldiers killed 300 Sioux at Wounded Knee, South Dakota. The **massacre** marked the end of the military campaign against Native peoples—but not of the struggle to reclaim their tribal lands.

Right: Members of the Oglala Sioux perform the Ghost Dance in 1890.

A "Civilized" Education

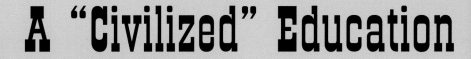

★ **Schools with a mission**

★ **Wipe out Native heritage**

In 1879, Colonel Richard Henry Pratt opened the Carlisle Indian Industrial School in Pennsylvania. He wanted to educate Native children so they could be **assimilated** into US society. Children were taken from their families and forced to live at the school. They were not allowed to speak their traditional languages or wear traditional clothes. Many schools worked in the same way. Residential schools such as these had terrible effects on Native children and their families. Many children died, were mistreated, and lost their Native heritage forever. In Canada, the government apologized for these schools in 2008.

Above: Native American children wear formal "white" clothes during their schooling.

ONGOING STRUGGLE

★ **Legal cases continue**

★ **Fighting for rights**

The expansion of white settlement in the West still has effects today. In the late 1800s, Native nations were forced to agree to treaties with the US and Canadian governments, which the governments later broke. In the 1900s, Native nations began to use the law courts to try to regain rights to their traditional territory. Some successful cases gave the nations the rights to minerals found on their land. Other cases have still to be resolved. The Apache, for example, are trying to prevent mining in their traditional lands in Tonto National Forest (right).

GLOSSARY

adobe A kind of clay used as a building material

assimilated Absorbed into another culture

beadwork Decoration formed with colored beads

colonial Related to the colonies ruled by an empire

convert To change one's religious beliefs

credit A system in which people purchase goods or services but pay for them in the future

displaced Forced to leave one's home, usually by war or natural disaster

economy The financial system of a region, including the manufacture and distribution of goods and services and the means by which people pay for them

elders People who hold a senior position in a tribe because of their age or achievements

fur trapper Someone who hunts animals for their skins

homestead A house with an area of land

interpreter Someone who translates what someone says into another language

massacre The brutal killing of many people

militia A military force made up of armed civilians

missionaries People who try to promote a religion in a foreign land

mountain man Someone who lived and worked in the wilderness beyond human settlement

negotiate To solve disagreements by discussion

nomadic Describing people with no fixed home who instead move from place to place

persecution Hostility toward, and ill-treatment of, an individual or group of people because of their race, religion, or other beliefs

reservations Areas of land given to Native American nations

resources Things that can be put to use, such as minerals, crops, or wood from trees

sacrificed Gave up something valuable to achieve a purpose

seer A person who has visions of the future

shaman A person who claims to be able to contact the spirit world and who practices healing

tipis Conical tents made from a framework of poles covered by skins or canvas

treaties Agreements between two or more groups or nations

vision Something seen in a dream, especially as part of a religious experience

---

April 30: The United States buys the vast Louisiana Territory from France under the Louisiana Purchase.

May 28: The Indian Removal Act authorizes the forced removal of the "Five Civilized Tribes" from the East.

The US Army goes to war with the Seminole of Florida; most of the Seminole move west, though some resist until 1855

July 24: The Mormons settle Salt Lake City in Utah Territory; they come into contact with Ute and Paiute.

1803 1804 1830 1834 1835 1838 1847 1848

President Thomas Jefferson sends expeditions to explore the West.

June 30: The government creates Indian Territory, now Oklahoma, as a home for Native peoples displaced from the East.

Cherokee living in the East are forced by the US Army to travel to Indian Territory (modern Oklahoma) along the "Trail of Tears."

January 24: Gold is discovered in California, starting a gold rush that displaces many Native peoples in the region.

ON THE WEB

http://www.history.com/topics/native-american-history/native-american-cultures

A page from History.com about the different Native American cultures, with links and videos.

http://www.cherokee.org/AboutTheNation/History/TrailofTears/ABriefHistoryoftheTrailofTears.aspx

A page from the Cherokee Nation with a short history of their forced removal along the "Trail of Tears."

http://www.edweek.org/ew/projects/2013/native-american-education/history-of-american-indian-education.html

Gives a timeline detailing day and boarding schools in the United States and their effects.

http://wherearethechildren.ca/en/timeline/research/

Gives a timeline detailing residential schools in Canada and their effects.

BOOKS

Langley, Andrew. *The Plains Indian Wars 1864–1890* (Living Through). Heinemann, 2012.

Lowenstein, Tom, and Piers Vitebsky. *Native American Myths and Beliefs* (World Mythologies). Rosen Publishing Group, 2011.

Peppas, Lynn. *The Displacement of Native Peoples*. Crabtree Publishing, 2016.

Schwartz, Heather E. *Forced Removal: Causes and Effects of the Trail of Tears* (Cause and Effect). Capstone Press, 2015.

The Apache begin an armed struggle against the US Army that will continue until 1886.

May 10: The first transatlantic railroad line is completed at Promontory Point, Utah.

The discovery of gold in the Black Hills of Dakota attracts miners to land that is sacred to the Sioux.

The Dawes Act allows the government to claim a large area of land previously set aside for Native peoples.

1861   1868   1869   1872   1874   1876   1887 1890

April 29: The Treaty of Fort Laramie guarantees tribal lands for the Plains peoples and closes the Bozeman Trail.

July 6: In northern California, the Modoc begin a year-long fight against the US Army to avoid being moved to a reservation.

Lakota Sioux and their allies fight the US Army in the Great Sioux War. They are forced to surrender the following year.

US troops kill hundreds of Sioux at Wounded Knee in Montana, marking the end of military campaign against Native Americans.

INDEX